In the be

A book of 30 Bible readings and notes
to help you worship and pray

Rosemary Stokes and Tony Phelps-Jones

Published by Scripture Union, 207–209 Queensway, Bletchley, MK2 2EB, England.
Email: info@scriptureunion.org.uk
Internet: www.scriptureunion.org.uk

© Copyright all editions Causeway PROSPECTS
First published in 2006
ISBN 1 84427 218 4

All rights reserved. No part of this publication may be reproduced, stored in a retrieval system or transmitted, in any form or by any means electronic, mechanical, photocopying, recording or otherwise, without the prior permission of Scripture Union.

The right of Causeway PROSPECTS to be identified as owning this work has been asserted by their director Tony Phelps-Jones in accordance with the Copyright, Designs and Patents Act 1988.

Causeway PROSPECTS is a division of PROSPECTS for People with Learning Disabilities and their address is PO Box 351, Reading, RG30 4XQ. Phone 0118 9516 978. Email causeway@prospects.org.uk

About Causeway Prospects: Causeway PROSPECTS provides resource materials and training to equip churches for effective outreach and ministry among people with learning disabilities. It also runs holiday weekends and special ministry at Spring Harvest and the Keswick Convention.

British Library Cataloguing-in-Publication Data: a catalogue record for this book is available from the British Library.

Scripture portions are taken from The Holy Bible: English Version for the Deaf (published as the Easy-to-Read Version) © 2000 by the World Bible Translation Center, Inc. and used with permission. Internet: www.wbtc.com

Icons © Widgit Software Ltd 2002, developed by the Rebus Symbol Development Project, designed by Cate Detheridge and used with kind permission.

Cover design by David Lund Design: www.davidlund-design.com

Internal page layout by Creative Pages: www.creativepages.org.uk

Printed and bound in Great Britain by goodmanbaylis, The Trinity Press, Worcester, UK.

Scripture Union is an international charity working with churches in more than 130 countries providing resources to bring the good news about Jesus Christ to children, young people and families – and to encourage them to develop spiritually through the Bible and prayer. As well as a network of volunteers, staff and associates who run holidays, church-based events and school Christian groups, we produce a wide range of publications and support those who use our resources through training programmes.

Using this book

In the beginning and the other titles in this series are intended to help you to worship and pray. On each page there is a reading from the Bible, some thoughts and a prayer.

The readings are from the *Easy-to-Read Version* (ETRV), a very clear and simple translation of the Bible. The reading printed each day is quite short. A longer reading is also given if you would like to read more using your own Bible. There is a list of key words and their meanings near the back of the book.

Reading the Bible

The Bible, which is sometimes called the Word of God, is not really one book but a whole library of many books. The 66 books were written by many people who God spoke to at different times. At the front of the Bible you will find a list of the titles of all the books in the Bible and the page number where each book begins.

To help you find your way around such a big book, little groups of one or two sentences have been numbered, and then groups of those sentences have been collected into chapters.

So how do you find the one or two sentences that you want in the Bible? Let's say you want to find Matthew 5:5,6. That means you need to look in the book called Matthew, in chapter number 5 and verses 5 and 6.

You can find Matthew in the list of books at the front of the Bible. This tells you which page Matthew starts on. When you have turned to the beginning of Matthew you then search for chapter 5. Look down the page until you see the numbers 5 and 6. Those are the sentences (or verses) that you need.

When you do your Bible reading, try to spend a few extra minutes praying and worshipping. Praying is talking and listening to God. You can do this aloud or without using words. You can pray on your own or with friends. Worship is telling God how much you love him, through words or songs, or things you do. This can be singing in church, but it's a lot more than that. It's about enjoying the wonderful world God has made. It's about how we speak to each other. It's about how we live our lives.

As you pray you can:

 thank God for his goodness and his help;

 tell God how great he is, and that you love him;

 ask God to help you, your friends, your family and other people.

If you are a helper using this book with someone who does not read, you will find guidance notes at the end.

The *Easy-to-Read Version* of the Bible is available to buy from Causeway PROSPECTS.

In the beginning

1	The earth around us	7
2	Before the beginning	8
3	Day and night	9
4	Air and water	10
5	Land appears	11
6	Rivers, seas and lakes	12
7	Trees and flowers	13
8	Give me sunshine	14
9	New moon	15
10	Fish	16
11	Birds	17
12	Animals	18
13	People – a copy of God	19
14	Adam and Eve	20
15	Babies	21
16	People are important	22
17	Taking a rest	23

18	Praise the Lord!	24
19	God's rules	25
20	Look after it!	26
21	Trusting God	27
22	Breaking the rules	28
23	Being found out	29
24	Sent away	30
25	Only Noah was good	31
26	Noah's ark	32
27	Making the world good	33
28	God's promise	34
29	The earth is the Lord's	35
30	Praise the Lord!	36

1 The earth around us

God made the sky and earth. At first, the earth was completely empty; nothing was on the earth.
Genesis 1:1,2 (Full reading Genesis 1:1–3)

The Bible tells us that God made everything. Long ago when there was nothing, God wanted to make something beautiful to enjoy. He made the earth and he made the heavens – the sky and all the stars.

In the next few readings we will find out how he made them. As we think about the things God made, we will learn more about God. As we look at what God has made, we will see how beautiful God is.

Dear God, thank you for making the earth. Please help me to remember that it is your earth because you made it. Amen.

2 Before the beginning

Before the world began, the Word was there. The Word was there with God. The Word was God. He was there with God in the beginning.
John 1:1,2 (Full reading John 1:1–3)

Before we can think more about God making the earth, we have to answer a question: 'Where did God come from?'

'The Word' means Jesus. You might have heard people talking about 'The Living Word'. It's a name for Jesus. The Bible tells us that before the world began, God and Jesus were already there. Nobody made God. Nobody made Jesus. They have always been there.

What's more, God and Jesus will live for ever. They will always be there. The Bible calls that everlasting life or eternal life.

Dear God, thank you that we can trust in you when we pray because you are always going to be there. Amen.

3 Day and night

Then God said, 'Let there be light!' And light began to shine. God saw the light, and he knew it was good. Then God separated the light from the darkness.
Genesis 1:3,4 (Full reading Genesis 1:1–5)

Before God started making things, it was dark all the time. Then God made daytime when it is light and we can see. In the daylight we can see the things God has made and enjoy them. At night when it is dark outside we have streetlights to help us see. At home we push the light switch to make it bright inside the house.

Most people work in the day and sleep at night. But some people have to work at night, like doctors and nurses in hospital and policemen. Do you know anyone who works at night?

Dear God, please help people who have to work at night. Keep them safe and help them to sleep well when they get home. Amen.

4 Air and water

Then God said, 'Let there be air to separate the water into two parts!' ... God named the air 'sky'.
Genesis 1:6,8 (Full reading Genesis 1:6–8)

Air and water are very important indeed. Without them we would die. We need air to breathe. We need water to drink. People, animals and plants must have air and water. God knew that we would need them, so God made the sky. The air we breathe is from God.

We usually get water from taps or bottles. And we use water to make tea or coffee or cold drinks. Whenever you have a drink, remember God made the water and thank him.

Dear God, thank you for air and water. Thank you for giving us all the things we need to live. Amen.

5   Land appears

Then God said, 'Let the water under the sky be gathered together so the dry land will appear.' And it happened. God named the dry land 'earth'. And God named the water that was gathered together 'seas'. God saw this was good.
Genesis 1:9,10 (Full reading Genesis 1:9,10)

At first there was only water. Then God made land, lots of land. There are many countries in the world. Every country is different from the others. Some countries are very flat. Others have lots of mountains. Some countries are dry and look rather like a beach – brown and sandy. Other countries have lots of trees and grass and look much greener.

Think about the country you live in. Thank God for it.

Dear God, thank you for making the world, the sea and the land. Amen.

6 Rivers, seas and lakes

Then God said, 'Let the water under the sky be gathered together so the dry land will appear.' ... God named the dry land 'earth'. And God named the water that was gathered together 'seas'. God saw this was good.
Genesis 1:9,10 (Full reading Genesis 1:9,10)

It's nice when the sun shines, but we need the rain too. Without rain the grass and trees and flowers would not grow. The rain fills the streams and the rivers, and the rivers flow into the sea.

Can you remember the last time you were at the seaside or by a river or a lake? Did you enjoy watching the waves? Or seeing spray breaking on rocks? Or seeing the trees and sky reflected in a lake like a mirror?

God made these beautiful things for us to enjoy.

Dear God, please help me and my friends to look around and notice how beautiful everything is that you have made. Amen.

7 Trees and flowers

Then God said, 'Let the earth grow grass, plants that make grain, and fruit trees. The fruit trees will make fruit with seeds in it. And each plant will make its own kind of seed. Let these plants grow on the earth.' And it happened.
Genesis 1:11   (Full reading Genesis 1:11–13)

God made plants, trees and grass to grow on the land. There were lots of different plants and lots of different trees. He made fruit trees like apple trees, pear trees and plum trees. All the flowers and plants had seeds, so new flowers and seeds could grow. God made sure that the earth would always have flowers and trees for us to enjoy.

Do you have a favourite flower? Do you like the taste of apples or bananas? Remember that God made all these things.

Thank you, Lord, for making lots of different plants and trees and flowers. Please help me to say thank you for my food whenever I eat. Amen.

8 Give me sunshine

So God made the two large lights. God made the larger light to rule during the day. He made the smaller light to rule during the night. God also made the stars.
Genesis 1:16 (Full reading Genesis 1:14–17)

Do you like the feeling of warmth when the sun shines on you? Most people do. We need the sun to give us light and warmth.

Plants, trees and flowers need the sun too if they are to grow leaves and flowers and fruit.

Without the sun, the earth would be covered in ice. It would be too cold for us to live here.

Dear God, thank you for the sun, for its light and warmth. Thank you for putting the sun in just the right place so we can live here on the earth. Amen.

9 New moon

Then God said, 'Let there be lights in the sky. These lights will separate the days from the nights ... And they will be used to show the days and years. These lights will be in the sky to shine light on the earth.'
Genesis 1:14,15 (Full reading Genesis 1:14–16)

Here is something for you to try. On a clear evening, go out in the dark and look at the moon. Sometimes it's a big circle – a full moon. Other times it's a really thin crescent shape. We call that a new moon.

If you go out for several nights you can watch the slow change from new moon to full moon and back again. It always takes the same number of days. God made it like that to help people to count the days and years. God is in charge of time.

Dear God, help me to use my time well, doing things that will help other people and please you. Amen.

10 Fish

So God made the large sea animals. God made every living thing that moves in the sea. There are many different kinds of sea animals – and God made them all!
Genesis 1:21 (Full reading Genesis 1:20,21)

Have you ever seen a television programme about sea life? Perhaps you have been to a sea life centre. There are thousands of different kinds of fish. Fish come in all shapes and sizes and every colour you can imagine. Some fish are smaller than your little finger; some are even bigger than people.

Some fish are good to eat. Many people work as fishermen to catch the fish. Fishing is hard work and sometimes dangerous.

Lord, thank you for making so many different kinds of fish. Please keep fishermen safe in their work. Amen.

11 Birds

Then God said, 'Let the water be filled with many living things. And let there be birds to fly in the air over the earth.' ... God also made every kind of bird that flies in the sky. And God saw this was good.
Genesis 1:20,21 (Full reading Genesis 1:20,21)

Birds are amazing. There are swallows that fly thousands of miles every year to Africa and back. There are cormorants that can dive into a river and swim under water to catch fish.

In England the robin is one of the best known birds. Its orange-red breast makes it easy to spot in the garden.

Do you have a birdfeeder in your garden? You can get one at a garden centre. Birds need extra food in the winter and putting birdseed or nuts out will help them.

Father God, thank you for birds. Help me to learn more about the different birds, fish and animals you have made. Amen.

12 Animals

So God made every kind of animal. God made the wild animals, the tame animals, and all the small crawling things. And God saw this was good.
Genesis 1:25 (Full reading Genesis 1:24,25)

God had made the earth with lots of different plants. Now he wanted to make animals. Some animals live in wild places – in the countryside, in a forest or in the mountains. We might only see those animals in the zoo or on television.

If you visit a farm you might see cows, pigs or chickens. At home you might have a dog, cat or hamster. God made all these animals.

Dear God, thank you for every type of animal. Help us to be kind to them and care for them. Amen.

13 People – a copy of God

So God made people in his own image. God made people as a copy of himself. God made them male and female.
Genesis 1:27 (Full reading Genesis 1:26,27)

God made people 'as a copy' of himself. People don't look like God, so what does it mean to be a 'copy' of God?

God loves people. And God put love into people so they can love him, and love other people. God is a thinker, so he gave people minds to think and to work things out. God cares deeply about people. The way God made us means we can care deeply about people too.

Loving, thinking, caring. That's how God is. That's how God has made us people to be.

Dear God, thank you for making me as a copy of you. Help me to understand more about what that means. Amen.

14 Adam and Eve

So God made people in his own image. God made people as a copy of himself. God made them male and female.
Genesis 1:27 (Full reading Genesis 1:26,27)

God had made a good earth with lots of different plants and animals. Now God wanted someone to talk to and someone who could talk to him. So he made people. He made a man called Adam and a woman called Eve. God made a lovely garden for Adam and Eve to live in. They had everything they needed there. They had food to eat and water to drink. And every day God talked to them and they talked to God.

Lord, thank you that Adam and Eve could talk to you every day. Please help me to talk to you every day. Help me to listen to you too. Amen.

15 Babies

So God made people in his own image. God made people as a copy of himself. God made them male and female. God blessed them and said to them, 'Have many children.'
Genesis 1:27,28 (Full reading Genesis 1:27,28)

All the animals, fish and birds have ways of making babies. That way there are still plenty of them when the older ones die. Birds lay eggs and the chicks come out of the eggs.

Let's give thanks to God for families! Isn't it great to have older and younger people to know and love and belong to us? And let's give thanks for babies! Each one is a tiny miracle. They are God's way of putting new people on the earth.

Dear God, thank you for the gift of life. Please help mothers with new babies to look after them well. Amen.

16 People are important

Lord, I look at the heavens you made with your hands. I see the moon and stars you created ... But people are important to you! ... And you crowned them with glory and honour.
Psalm 8:3,5 (Full reading Genesis 1:1,3,5)

We have been learning about how God made everything. The Bible tells us about the man called King David. He lived a long time ago. King David knew that God made everything and he wrote songs praising God for all he had made.

Like King David we can look at everything in the world that God has made. How wonderful God is! But remember: people are very important to God. More important than everything else he has made. You are very important to God. He cares about you. God loves you just the way you are.

Dear God, I praise you because you are great. Thank you for making me special. Thank you that I am important to you. Amen.

17 Taking a rest

God finished the work he was doing. So on the seventh day God rested from his work.
Genesis 2:2 (Full reading Genesis 2:1–3)

God was very pleased with what he had made. He had made all that the earth needed. He did not need to make anything else.

God had a rest from working. That's what God wants us to do too. He knows that we are busy during the week going to work or doing jobs. God wants us to have a rest on Sundays. On Sundays we can go to church to worship God and to learn more about him.

Dear God, thank you that Sunday is a special day. Thank you that we can go to church to worship you. Help me to learn more about you. Amen.

18 Praise the Lord!

Angels above, praise the Lord from heaven! ... Sun and moon, praise the Lord! Stars and lights in the sky, praise him! ... Everything on earth, praise the Lord! Great sea animals in the oceans, praise the Lord!
Psalm 148:1,3,7 (Full reading Psalm 148:1,3,7,13)

What a lot of things and people are praising the Lord! The person who wrote this praise song is thinking about how God made the earth. Do you remember how God made the sun and moon and stars to give us day and night? Praise the Lord! He made trees and animals and birds so we can eat fruit and enjoy seeing wildlife. Praise the Lord! God made people like you and me. Praise the Lord! Can you write or say your own list about what God has made?

Lord God, I praise you. I want to add my praise to the praise of angels and all creation. Let everything in heaven and earth praise you! Amen.

19 God's rules

The Lord God said, 'You may eat from any tree in the garden. But you must not eat from the tree that gives knowledge about good and evil. If you eat fruit from that tree you will die!'
Genesis 2:16,17 (Full reading Genesis 2:16,17)

God made a wonderful home for Adam and Eve to live in. They could grow what they liked and pick and eat their favourite fruit. There was just one rule. Adam and Eve must not touch one special tree. God told them that if they did touch the special tree they would die. God did not explain his rule. He wanted Adam and Eve to trust him and to do what he said.

It's the same with us. God wants us to trust him and do what he says. God knows what is best for us.

Lord God, please help me to trust you. Help me to choose to do the right thing. Amen.

20 Look after it!

The Lord God put the man in the garden of Eden to work the soil and take care of the garden.
Genesis 2:15 (Full reading Genesis 2:15–17)

God made a beautiful world full of plants, animals, trees and birds. Then God made people. God told people to take care of what he had made.

Perhaps you have heard people talking about conservation. That's another word for looking after the world. Looking after what God has made is an important job.

What could you do? Here are a few ideas. You could plant flowers in your garden to help insects. Save water by turning the tap off while you brush your teeth. Put used bottles, cans and paper in the recycling collection.

Talk to your friends or family about other ideas for taking care of God's world.

Dear God, thank you for making a beautiful world. Please show me how I can help to look after it. Amen.

21 Trusting God

The snake was the most clever of all the wild animals that the Lord God had made. The snake wanted to trick the woman. The snake ... said, 'Woman, did God really tell you that you must not eat from any tree in the garden?'
Genesis 3:1 (Full reading Genesis 3:1–4)

God gave Adam and Eve a rule to obey. They could eat anything in the garden except the fruit from one tree. Then along came the snake (another word for the devil). The snake asked Eve a question. Eve began to wish God had not given them his rule. She did not trust God to know best. We call this 'doubt'.

Sometimes the devil tries to make us doubt God. We must remember that God made us. He loves us and cares for us. We can trust him to know what is best.

Dear Lord, I know I can trust you. Please help me never to doubt you. Amen.

22 Breaking the rules

The woman saw ... the fruit was good to eat. And it was exciting that the tree would make her wise. So the woman took fruit from the tree and ate it. Her husband was there with her, so she gave some of the fruit to him and he ate it.
Genesis 3:6 (Full reading Genesis 3:4–6)

What a bad day! The snake tempted Eve and Eve doubted God. There were so many lovely things for Eve to eat. But she took some of the fruit that God said she could not have. Eve gave Adam some of the fruit and he ate it too. Now they had both done what God told them not to do.

We call wrong things like this 'sin'. Sin is doing anything which makes God unhappy. It makes us feel bad inside too.

Dear God, please help me not to do bad things. Help me always to do things that please you. Amen.

23 Being found out

The man said, 'The woman you made for me gave me fruit from that tree. So I ate it.' Then the Lord God said to the woman, 'What have you done?' The woman said, 'The snake tricked me. He fooled me and I ate the fruit.'
Genesis 3:12,13 (Full reading Genesis 3:11–13)

Adam and Eve had done something wrong. They had sinned. They were ashamed. They were afraid of God and they tried to hide. But God knows everything. No one can hide from him.

When Adam was found out, he said that Eve made him do it. Then Eve said the snake made her do it.

When we do wrong things we must not say someone else made us do it. The best thing is to tell the truth – every time.

Lord Jesus, please help me always to tell the truth. When I make mistakes please help me to own up. Amen.

24 Sent away

The Lord God forced the man to leave the garden. Then he put Cherub angels at the entrance to the garden to protect it.
Genesis 3:24 (Full reading Genesis 3:23,24)

Adam and Eve had sinned. They had not obeyed God's rules. Now God was sad and hurt by what they had done. God made them leave the beautiful garden. Adam and Eve were no longer God's special friends. Their sin kept them away from God. Adam and Eve would have to work hard to grow their food.

This was all because they did not trust God enough. They sinned. We sometimes do wrong things that keep us away from God. To show we are God's friends, we should do good things.

Dear God, I'm sorry for the wrong things I do. Please help me only to do good things. Amen.

25 Only Noah was good

The Lord saw that the people on the earth were very evil. The Lord saw that people thought only about evil things all the time ... But there was one man on earth that pleased the Lord – Noah.
Genesis 6:5,8 (Full reading Genesis 6:5,6,8)

After Adam and Eve left the garden they had children. Then their children had children. There were many, many people on the earth. They knew about God but they chose to do bad things instead of good things. They thought bad things and this made them behave badly. In the end God wished he had not made people at all. He decided to get rid of them.

But there was one man called Noah, who talked to God and kept God's rules. Noah always did the right thing even when no one else did.

Dear God, help me to remember Noah and do only good things today. Amen.

26 Noah's ark

... build a boat for yourself. Make rooms in the boat ... And you, your sons, your wife, and your sons' wives will all go into the boat. Also, you must find two of every living thing on the earth.
Genesis 6:14,18,19 (Full reading Genesis 6:14,18–21)

God told Noah exactly what to do. Noah did just what God said, even when it was very hard. Noah did not understand everything God told him, but Noah trusted God. When Noah's friends laughed at him he still trusted God. Noah did not doubt God.

What about us? We need to trust God. We need to do the things God wants. God will help us. God will give us people to help us. Think of someone who helps you know more about God.

Dear God, help me to know what you want me to do. Help me to live my life in a good way. Thank you for friends who help me. Amen.

27 Making the world good

Water flooded the earth for 40 days. The water began rising and lifted the boat off the ground ... Every living thing on earth died.
Genesis 7:17,21 (Full reading Genesis 7:17–23)

When Noah's boat, the ark, was ready it rained non-stop for nearly six weeks. No wonder there was a flood! Noah's boat and the people and animals inside it floated safely on the water. But everything else on the earth died. It was God's way of making his world good again. God took all the bad away.

God always has a plan for making things good again, even today. In Noah's time God's plan was a big flood. For us today God's plan is Jesus. You can read more about Jesus in the book *God gives new life*.

Dear God, thank you for your plan to make things good again. Thank you for Noah's faith, and thank you for Jesus. Amen.

28 God's promise

[God said] 'When I see this rainbow, I will remember the agreement between me and you and every living thing on the earth. That agreement says that a flood will never again destroy all life on the earth.'
Genesis 9:15 (Full reading Genesis 9:11–17)

After six weeks the rain stopped. At last, after more time passed, God told Noah to send the animals out of the ark. Noah and his family came out as well. They had to start all over again to build a house and make a garden and a town.

God promised never to flood the earth again. He gave us a sign to help us remember his promise – the rainbow. When you see a rainbow, remember God keeps his promises. We can trust him. We should be people who keep our promises too.

Father God, thank you for your promises. Thank you that we can trust in you. Help me to keep the promises I make. Amen.

29 The earth is the Lord's

The earth and everything on it belong to the Lord. The world and all its people belong to him.
Psalm 24:1 (Full reading Psalm 24:1,2)

This is one of King David's praise songs. King David is remembering that God made everything. God made everything for us to enjoy, but we must always remember that the earth belongs to God first.

It is good to get out for a walk or a drive in the countryside sometimes. Next time you are out, thank God for the things you see. Thank God for the trees and flowers. Thank God for rocky mountains and green fields. Thank God for cows and sheep, for birds and fish.

Dear God, thank you for making such a wonderful world. Help my friends and me to see more of your beauty in the world around us. Amen.

30 Praise the Lord!

Praise God for the great things he does! Praise him for all his greatness! ... Every living thing, praise the Lord! Praise the Lord!
Psalm 150:2,6 (Full reading Psalm 150:2–6)

This is a great song of praise. When people begin to understand what God has done, they want to praise him. When people see great mountains or a beautiful lake, they want to praise him. When people see a tree or a flower in bloom they want to praise God.

This song is a call to praise God any way you can. You can praise God with a drum or a shaker. You can praise God with singing and clapping.

For your prayer today say or sing these words: Hallelujah, praise the Lord! Hallelujah, praise the Lord! Let everything that has breath praise the Lord!

Key words

Amen — We usually say this at the end of prayers and it means, 'That's my prayer too'.

Conservation — Looking after the world around us. Looking after the things God made.

Crescent — A thin curved shape like a new moon.

Doubt — When you're not sure if something is true.

Eternal — Lasting for ever. It never ends.

Faith — Believing that God will keep his promises.

Image — A copy or a reflection (like in a mirror).

Lord — The one in charge. Another word for God.

Obey — To do what you are told to do.

Praise — To tell God (or a person) how good they are.

Pray — To talk to God or Jesus about things.

Promise — Something you say you will do for somebody.

Psalm — A song written to God.

Recycling — Using something again to save waste.

Sin/sins Things people do that make God sad and hurt other people.

Tempt Try to make someone do something bad.

Worship Telling God how much you love him through words or songs or things you do.

Notes for carers and helpers

These Bible guides are designed to help a wide range of people who need extra help. It's impossible to tailor Bible notes to fit everyone's needs. But our hope is that many who have some level of visual or intellectual disability or just need a simpler approach can be helped to pray and read the Bible regularly through this series.

Some people will be able to use these notes without any help from others. But if you are the carer or helper of someone needing some assistance with using them, here are a few pointers which may be useful to you.

Before you begin, ask the Holy Spirit to help communicate the main thought from each reading and note to the person you are reading with. God through the Holy Spirit can communicate on levels that we cannot! Part of the Holy Spirit's role is to make Jesus real to people and you are working in partnership with him.

Make sure you have the person's full attention before starting to read. Think about how you can eliminate auditory or visual distractions in the environment such as TV or other people's conversations. Try to find a quiet place. Use eye contact to maintain good connection.

Read slowly and clearly, pausing where suitable. Facial expressions, hand and body movements can all help to underline the meaning of the material. Encourage whatever response is appropriate, particularly in prayer and praise.

Use your knowledge of the person to assess how much is being understood, how much clarification might be needed and how best to make applications more relevant.

Make your time together an opportunity for learning and fellowship for both of you.

Other titles in the Bible Prospects series:

Being like Jesus

God gives new life

Moses, man of God

Songs of praise

The first Christians

The story of Christmas

The story of Easter

Bible Prospects on audio A number of these titles are available as audio CDs by mail order from Causeway PROSPECTS PO Box 351, Reading, RG30 4XQ. Phone 0118 9516 978. Email causeway@prospects.org.uk

Scripture Union produces a wide range of Bible reading notes for people of all ages and Bible-based material for small groups. SU publications are available from Christian bookshops. For information and to request free samples and a free catalogue of Bible resources:

- ✧ phone SU's mail order line: local rate number 08450 706006
- ✧ email info@scriptureunion.org.uk
- ✧ fax 01908 856020
- ✧ log on to www.scriptureunion.org.uk
- ✧ write to SU Mail Order, PO Box 5148, Milton Keynes MLO, MK2 2YX